FIRST CLASS CREDIT

FIRST CLASS CREDIT

ASHLEY MASSENGILL

StoryTerrace®

Text Angela Sayre, on behalf of Story Terrace

Design Adeline Media, London

Copyright © Ashley Massengill

First print December 2018

www.StoryTerrace.com

Disclaimer: The author assumes no responsibility for your interpretation of this book. This book is not considered to be legal advice. Please consult with an attorney for legal advice.

CONTENTS

1. ABOUT THE AUTHOR   11

2. CASH IS KING, CREDIT IS
   POWER   21

3. CREDIT LAWS AND
   FINANCIAL AGENCIES   33

4. HOW FICO SCORES ARE
   CALCULATED   39

5. HOW TO READ YOUR
   CREDIT REPORT   49

6. DISPUTING TECHNIQUES   55

7. BUILDING AND
   REBUILDING POSITIVE
   CREDIT   65

8. CALL TO ACTION   75

9. CHANGING STEREOTYPES   79

10. SUCCESS STORIES   85

1

ABOUT THE AUTHOR

I never considered myself financially responsible as a young adult. I grew up in Baltimore in a single-parent home with a mother who also wasn't taught the importance of being financially responsible. Credit was never even mentioned in the household when I was a child. I saw my mom paying cash for everything, so I assumed that was the way to pay for everything. I started racking up debt as soon as I graduated high school. I got my first credit card offer in the mail the same month that I turned eighteen. I applied and was instantly approved for $150 from Credit One Bank. I used it to buy my first cell phone from Sprint and never made any payments on the card. I thought, "My credit score doesn't really matter. I can use cash in the future to buy whatever I need." Boy, was I wrong.

I remember going to the dealership to buy my dream car: an Acura TL with the technology package. I was so excited about getting this car because I was bringing a large down payment to the table. I will never forget the look that the car salesman gave me when he came back with my credit score. He told me that even with me putting down $15,000, eight banks had denied me financing. And the one bank who did agree to extend me the loan was charging me a 15.99 interest rate. I was going to be paying almost double for this loan if I wanted to leave the lot with that car. I had over 42 negative accounts on my credit.

Embarrassed is an understatement. My pride told me that I was well-spoken and could easily talk my way into a good deal. But reality set in, and I realized that my poor financial decisions in life had taken away my ability to negotiate. Credit was not something that I'd learned about in school or at home. In fact, it's something that most people don't learn about at all until they arrive in a situation much like mine, or where they need a credit card for a family emergency or a reasonable loan for a mortgage. Up until that point, I had no idea that my credit score was in the 400s. I knew that I didn't have stellar credit because I didn't finance a lot of things, but I had no clue it was that horrible.

This is when I learned the importance of credit versus cash. I had always believed that if you had so much cash in your hand, it would be easier to buy or finance whatever you wanted. I learned when I left the car dealership that day with my car that they didn't see me as someone with a large down payment coming to buy a car. They saw me as someone trying to finance a car with a 499 credit score. I didn't know that unless you're paying the car completely off, you still need a good credit score along with your down payment or you will have an unbearable interest rate. Which may or may not break the deal for your budget and planning.

My mother also had bad credit. Much like my siblings and me, she grew up in a household where no one understood credit and how it affected your buying power into adulthood. My mom was always renting and didn't feel like she needed credit because she wasn't looking to buy a home. As she got older, she realized that she was throwing a lot of money away as a renter and would rather put her money towards something that she could actually own. I spoke with my mother after buying my car and was shocked to hear that she had been repairing her own credit. She had gotten her score from the 400s to the mid-700s in less than two years. I was floored when she logged in to her credit monitoring account and showed me her FICO Scores. I thought if she could do this, surely, I could do it too. Six months before her 50th birthday, she was able to accomplish her goal of becoming a first-time homeowner.

I was a little skeptical at first. Debt and poor credit can make you feel like you're at the end of the world with no hope of getting back on track. Every minor setback and misstep lowers your score. However, after listening to my mother and doing my own research, I realized that I could repair and build my credit myself with a little determination, research, and patience. I was tired of throwing money away to high interest rates, so I began asking my mom for insight in how she brought her credit scores up. I remember seeing her progress before she bought her home and thinking, *wow*. This is real, and we can really change our lives with this knowledge. A lot of people think that you need to wait seven years for debt to fall off of your credit report, but there are steps you can take to raise your score—like we both did—in a short amount of time.

By repairing her credit and teaching me where to look, I began taking the necessary steps to take back control of my credit. It is something that we both still actively do as we move into the first class lifestyle that we've always dreamed of. I started repairing my credit in March 2016. By June 2016, I had gone from a 499 to a 577 credit score. Fast forward to September 2016, and my credit score was a 721. I was completely blown away by the time frame. I could not believe that these were my actual credit scores. This was the first time in my entire life that I was able to say that I had excellent credit. I was so excited that I posted my results on social media to friends and family. Immediately my in-box was flooded with hundreds of people messaging me, asking how I achieved such a great credit score. Realizing that you have bad credit can be a huge wake-up call. There is often a lack of conversation about how to prioritize the financial habits of needs versus wants, much less building credit to help you achieve a desirable financial future.

Not everyone is willing to openly share their struggles, especially online. But I knew this was something I could not just sit on. I felt like I opened the floodgates to everyone who had wondered or felt ashamed about their own credit scores. Everyone wanted my help in raising their personal credit scores simply because I had shared my journey.

At first I said "no" because repairing other people's credit wasn't my job. Plus, I didn't have the time with my full-time job to do this for others. So, for about four months, I continued to say "no" to people asking to hire me or help them repair their credit. Instead, I would pass out the tools and sample letters that had helped me in my first few months.

Within a few months, I realized that there was a huge need for this. I started receiving feedback from everyone about their own amazing results from my help, and I began thinking about credit repair as a full-time business. Everyone needs money and credit to thrive. I could help them do just that. But I was immediately conscious of how much work I had to do to become financially literate, and I saw the lack of financial knowledge being shared around me. So, I decided to quit my full-time job to focus solely on helping others.

I launched my credit repair company, AM/PM Credit Repair, in February 2017. I quit my full-time job at the post office in March 2017.

I launched this business to empower everyday people, like myself, to take charge of their future and not get run over by financial institutions that benefit from us not knowing how the system works. At AM/PM Credit Repair, we specialize in financial literacy, building positive credit, and helping consumers dispute inaccurate, duplicate, and/or unverifiable items in their credit reports that are causing a decrease in their credit scores. I decided to write this book because there were people who just couldn't afford my services, along with the monthly payment to continue those services. And I didn't want to leave anyone behind. Each one, teach one.

If you're not familiar with my name, you're probably wondering: "Where did the name AM/PM Credit Repair come from?" A lot of people assume that it means my company will work on your credit all day and all night. But it's actually the initials of my husband and myself. It also goes along with our motto: "The difference in your credit will be like day and night." We have had success in helping thousands of consumers repair their credit. By following the strategies in this book, we hope that you too will find success in your journey.

2

CASH IS KING, CREDIT IS POWER

Y our credit scores are a vital part of your credit health. They are the determining factor in whether or not lenders will extend credit to you and what the interest rate will be, should they decide to do so. So what exactly is a credit score and why does it matter? Whether you want to apply for a credit card, auto loan, or mortgage, lenders want to know your credit score first so they can understand the risk they will be taking on by loaning you money. Your credit reports help lenders assess that risk since it summarizes your personal credit profile and offers a financial snapshot of your life at that particular point.

By reading this book, you are saying that you want knowledge about your credit to determine your own financial future. That's a powerful step to independence and financial health. You will learn how your FICO credit scores are calculated, how to find and dispute errors, build positive credit, and maintain it. FICO Scores are used in 90% of all credit decisions. They are kind of like the X-rays of your past and most recent financial behaviors.

After sticking to the plan outlined throughout this book, I was able to refinance my car loan at a 4% interest rate. You have to keep in mind that having a lower credit score means lenders can take advantage of you. For example, say you want to buy a car, like I did. You go into the dealership, and they immediately run your credit report. If you have great credit, the first bank will pick you up and say, "Yes, we want that person. They have proven creditworthiness and will be able to pay us back on time." If you have bad or poor credit, your credit may be pulled up to ten times by ten different lenders in a single day. And even though you are being denied by several lenders, the credit bureaus are still being paid every single time a new lender pulls your credit file. Whether you get approved or not they still get paid. This is one of the many examples of how the credit bureaus make more money off of you having poor credit than they do with you having great credit.

It doesn't matter how much cash you have in your pockets or saved in your banking account if you need a loan for a larger purchase. Building a better credit score offers more than just a better interest rate or approval on a car or mortgage loan, it provides you the opportunity to save for emergency funds or help out a family member by being able to cosign on their loans.

One of my favorite success stories is of a client who rebuilt their credit with the help of AM/PM Credit Repair and was able to turn a terrible situation into owning a brand new car. This client's car would not start and could not be easily fixed. Because of her good credit report, she was able to walk into a Toyota dealership and get a car that same day with no money down, a good interest rate, and even a few months until her first official payment was due. That's the power of credit. Her lenders knew she had established a healthy financial history and would continue to do so, so they helped her during what would have otherwise been a truly stressful scenario of having no transportation and zero help in getting a new car.

If you still aren't sure of how important good credit is, just be aware that society is becoming increasingly dependent on using credit to make all purchases and decisions. It's more than just getting credits cards or loans. More and more businesses make the case that you must have good credit before they will extend their services to you. In short, here are some of the reasons you want good credit, what bad versus good credit means to you, and how bad credit significantly raises your financial burden:

Bad Credit

- **It affects where you live and how much you pay**: Do you want to live in a certain neighborhood or school zone? You may not have much of a choice with bad credit. Even if you are not buying a home right now, landlords will use your credit to decide whether or not to rent to you. Your lease is considered a loan. It doesn't matter how much a landlord likes you; goodwill does not translate into making payments on time, and no one likes nagging anyone into paying. Don't risk being denied the apartment or home you want.

- **Limited mobility**: There are causes for emergency all the time. If you've ever lived through a natural disaster like Hurricane Katrina or Hurricane Harvey, fires, or sudden moves, you likely quickly understood that having no cash or credit on hand is devastating.

- **It affects other monthly bills**: Have you ever paid a high fee to turn on your utilities? You likely have bad credit. It may sound shocking, but companies providing cable, telephone or cell phone services, water, and electricity think of your services as a loan too. You can be charged high fees if it looks like you are often late or missing payments.

- **Bad credit will prevent you from getting credit cards or loans**: Unless you have enough money to pay the full price of the car, then, like me, a great down payment will get you nowhere. As my experience proved, poor credit means a higher interest rate and, therefore, a higher car note to pay each month. The same goes with credit cards—poor credit means low limits and high interest rates.

- **Bad credit makes your auto insurance significantly more expensive:** While this is illegal in most states, it can and does still happen. Car insurers can drastically raise your insurance or deny auto coverage based on credit, which in turn negatively impacts the quality of life for any person dependent on a car for work.

- **It can affect your job search:** Sixty percent of all employers pull credit reports before offering employment. If you haven't demonstrated financial responsibility, a prospective employer might believe your debt is too high for the salary offered or may pass you over altogether, especially in financial or managerial-related roles. Some states look at this type of screening as discriminatory. However, it is 100% legal to deny employment in many states based on your credit profile.

- **It can impact your health:** Not being able to make payments because they are too high, thanks to interest rates, and the overall emotional shame of poor credit can cause additional stress to your life.

- Good credit offers you lower interest rates and the chance to save more money each month, which says enough right there.

- Good credit gives you a better chance for loan approvals and the opportunity to have the lifestyle you desire.

★ ★ ★

There are some myths about credit that I would like to clear up as well. One is that checking your credit hurts your score. You can check your own credit reports/scores as many times as you like without ever losing any points. This is what you would call a "soft inquiry." Soft inquiries are not included in your credit report. However, if a lender were to pull your credit that would be considered a "hard inquiry," which will result in your score decreasing. While hard inquiries are sometimes necessary, they should be kept to a minimum. You shouldn't be applying for any unnecessary loans or loans that you don't have a great chance of being approved for. It is also important to remember that hard inquiries only make up 10% of your FICO Score and only affect your credit for twelve months. After the one-year mark, hard inquiries are no longer factored into your score. However, they will still remain on your credit profile for 24 months from the date that your credit was pulled.

Another myth is that major events, like bankruptcy or foreclosure, mean that you will have bad credit forever. It's true that these are not desirable situations, but bankruptcy filing can only remain on your credit report for ten years and foreclosures for seven years. A lot of creditors and lenders will gauge how well you handle your finances post-bankruptcy, so even taking the initial steps as stated in this book will help get you into a healthier financial mode before that ten-year period is over. These types of events can cause your credit scores to drop by up to 220 points.

Also, it may be surprising, but credit scores aren't automatically taken on by your spouse or partner, even if you share the same last name. It is important to maintain your own positive credit score in case of unforeseen events, like getting divorced or being widowed. If you only use one spouse's credit and either of those life events happen, then you would have to start at the bottom and rebuild your credit.

There are myths that I'm even happier to dispel, like not being able to remove inaccuracies. One of our first steps in credit repair is finding errors in your credit report and investigating them so that they are corrected. This can be cleared up, as we will cover in *Chapter 6: Disputing Techniques.*

One of my favorite myths is that paying collection accounts off boosts your credit score and automatically removes it from your credit report. This is absolutely false. This is something that we hear everyday from new enrollees: "I paid that debt. I don't understand why it's still showing up," or "I don't

understand why my score didn't go up after I paid it off."
Once an account goes into collection, nothing you do can
make it positive again. It must be completely removed as if it
never existed to help your credit score.

Another myth is that once an account is removed
from your credit report, you no longer owe that debt. One
hundred percent false. You will always owe the balance on
that account. Having it removed just hides it from potential
lenders/creditors. So if you try to get financing, then they
would never know that those debts even existed. Unless it's
a bankruptcy. Bankruptcies are also reported on a website
called www.pacer.gov and cannot be disputed there. Which
is where mortgage lenders will go and find out about any
bankruptcies filed within the last seven to ten years. It doesn't
automatically disqualify you from getting a mortgage. I have
lots of clients who have become homeowners less than five
years after filing for bankruptcy. But this is just a fair warning
that mortgage lenders do have access to that information. It is
your responsibility to fulfill each contract with your creditors.
But depending on the creditors, legal action may never be
taken. For example, I had 42 negative remarks on my credit
when I started repairing it. At the time in 2016, 90% of
those accounts were still within the statute of limitations. But
only one out of 42 creditors filed a judgement against me,
which was settled out of court for $2,000. It's a risk that you
personally take when you decide not to fulfill those obligations
once they're deleted from your credit reports.

Creditors can sue you forever, as long as you don't pay the debt—this is also a myth. Creditors can only take legal against you if your accounts are within the statute of limitations. The statute of limitations varies for all 50 states. A quick Google search will let you know what the time frame for legal action is within each state. An important factor to know is that, *by law*, if creditors are contacting you outside of the statute of limitations, they must let you know within the letter they sent in an attempt to collect that they have no grounds to pursue any legal action. Also, keep in mind that making any kind of payment will *reset* that debt. So, a creditor who had no legal grounds to sue you can now take you to court and have your wages garnished.

These are just a few myths that I wanted to name. Just in case you've heard these myths as much as I have, you'll know that they hold absolutely no weight.

3

CREDIT LAWS AND FINANCIAL AGENCIES

Educating yourself as a consumer is one of your most powerful tools. When repairing your credit, let's discuss a few laws or financial terms you should be aware of that describe your consumer credit rights, including how credit is extended to you and how it is reported throughout other credit bureaus.

This is a short list, which isn't made to overwhelm you, but rather to inform you on where we find the information and the exact tools we have available to restore credit. These are the financial institutions and acronyms you should be familiar with. When it comes to repairing credit, knowing about these acronyms and agencies will help, especially when it comes to your paper trail and disputing inaccuracies.

- **FCRA**: Fair Credit Reporting Act is a federal law that regulates how consumer reporting agencies use your information. This law entitles you to a free copy of your credit report annually, thanks to the FACTA (described below). Additionally, this law gives consumers the right to dispute inaccurate or erroneous information in their credit reports.

- **FCBA**: Fair Credit Billing Act is a United States federal law enacted in 1974 as an amendment to the Truth in Lending Act (15 U.S.C. § 1601). Its purpose is to protect consumers from unfair billing practices and to prove a mechanism for addressing billing errors in "open end" credit accounts, such as a credit card or charge card accounts. This is great when you need a third party to help mediate when you are having trouble getting to the bottom of your issues or items lenders are willing to let go of that negatively affect your credit scoring.

- **FACTA**: Fair and Accurate Credit Transactions Act is an amendment to FCRA (Fair Credit Reporting Act) that was primarily added to protect consumers from identity theft.

- **FDCPA**: Fair Debt Collection Practices Act prohibits debt collectors from using abusive, unfair, or deceptive practices to collect from you.

- **HIPAA**: Health Insurance Portability and Accountability Act of 1996 is United States legislation that proves data privacy and security provisions for safeguarding medical information.

- **CROA**: Credit Repair Organizations Act is Title IV of the Consumer Credit Protection Act. It prohibits untrue or misleading representations and requires certain affirmative disclosures in the offering or sale of "credit repair" services. CROA bars companies offering credit repair services from demanding advance payment, requires that credit repair contracts be in writing, and gives consumers certain contract cancellation rights.

- **FTC**: Federal Trade Commission is an independent agency of the United States government, established in 1914 by the Federal Trade Commission Act. Its principal mission is the promotion of consumer protection and the elimination and prevention of anticompetitive business practices, such as coercive monopoly.

- **BBB**: Better Business Bureau, founded in 1912, is a nonprofit organization focused on advancing marketplace trust and consists of 112 independently incorporated local BBB organizations in the United States.

Another important note is knowing where to find your free annual credit report. There is only one website authorized by federal law to provide free annual credit reports for consumers, and it can be found at AnnualCreditReport.com. Be weary of other companies offering free reports or misleading claims.

4

HOW FICO SCORES
ARE CALCULATED

The credit rating system can be complex and confusing. Studies have found that most people are overwhelmed with figuring out their credit scores and are often confused by the language of credit ratings. I understand that completely and will try to break down your FICO Score as simply as possible.

FICO is an acronym for Fair Isaac Corporation, the company that created the first credit scoring model in 1956. FICO is the original and most widely used credit score by lenders that determines your creditworthiness (whether or not you'll be approved for that loan you're applying for), and is typically determined by the FICO Score 8 model for mortgages and the FICO Auto Score for cars.

Base FICO Scores range from 300–850 and help lenders assess your likelihood of not paying back large borrowed sums in the future. The FICO Auto Score (and other industry specific scores) focus specifically on the likelihood of you paying back a credit obligation in that field. It will be judged heavily by how you used car loans in the past as well. An industry specific score ranges from 250–900. If you are seeking other types of credit, such as personal loans, student loans, retail loans, or other types of credit, then focus on the FICO Score 8.

Credit scoring models typically calculate the same factors contained in your credit reports. While there are many bureaus out there, there are three nationally accredited main bureaus to watch that house credit histories on most of us: Equifax, Experian, and TransUnion. Your three credit scores/reports from these bureaus are beneficial to know because these reports are how lenders will determine your creditworthiness when approving or denying you loans. You'll notice that each bureau interprets scores differently and applies their own risk criteria. If, say, you notice one score is significantly less than the other, you would need to pull the bureau's report to see where a negative mark is impacting your score.

In order for your FICO Score to be calculated, you generally must have at least one account open for six months or longer and at least one account that has been reported to the credit bureau within the last six months. If you haven't started building credit yet and have no negative remarks either, your credit scores will be zero or nonexistent. It's important to note that as your information changes from, say, disputes or new lines of credit, your current score will change. It's important to monitor your credit reporting as you build your credit because your score could go up or down in a matter of days from mistakes and inaccuracies.

The FICO Scores are broken down into five categories, which are as follows:

- **35% Payment History**: This is determined by on-time and late payments. It is the most heavily weighted factor in your credit history, so paying your monthly bills by the due date is a very important element to building and/or restoring your credit.

- **30% Credit Utilization**: This section is calculated by your revolving credit and your available credit versus your credit limits (credit cards). The rule of thumb is to keep your balances below 30% of your spending limit. The more you spend past 30% of your available limit, the more your credit scores will decrease. This is the second most heavily weighted factor in your FICO Score. You'll see this come up more in *Chapter 7: Repairing and Building Positive Credit*.

- **15% Age of Credit History**: This is the average age of *all* of your reflecting accounts. Good or bad. For example, if you have five accounts and all of them are five years old, your average age of history will be five years. Now let's say that you add two *new* accounts today, your age of credit history just went from 5 years to 3.8 years. The older your accounts, the healthier your credit score will be. Long standing positive accounts represent financial stability and low risks to lenders.

- **10% Types of Credit**: FICO takes into consideration your mixture of credit in this section. Mortgages, student loans, credit cards, auto loans, and retail accounts are a few examples of having a good credit mixture. Creditors want to see that you are able to manage multiple types of credit responsibly. You don't need to apply for all of these accounts. Just make sure that you have a mixture of revolving and installment loans. You also don't want to apply for cards that you don't plan on using. This will result in your account being closed or your credit limit being decreased. If you do not wish to use your card frequently, using it at least once every 3 months will still keep it active.

- **10% Inquiries**: Opening too many new accounts within a short amount of time will affect your score negatively. This section of your FICO Score is based on how many new credit accounts you've opened in a short period of time. Hard credit inquiries, which can happen when you apply for a credit card or loan, can hurt your score, especially if there are several occuring in a short period of time. When applying for a mortgage or other loan, it's good practice to not open new accounts within six months prior to application.

* * *

It is also important to note what is *not* in your FICO Score, as it can put you at ease. FICO Scores do not consider the following:

- Your race, color, religion, national origin, sex, or marital status
- Age (other types of scores may consider age, but not FICO)
- Where you live
- Any interest being charged on a particular credit card or other account
- Criminal background
- Any information that is not proven to be predictive of future credit performance
- Whether or not you are actively, or have a history of, participating in any credit counseling or credit repair of any kind

Basic scoring ranges are as follows:
- **Base FICO Score**: 300–850
- **Experian Plus Score**: 330–830
- **Equifax Credit Score**: 280–850
- **TransUnion TransRisk**: 300–850
- **VantageScore**: 300–850

* * *

The average person falls in the mid-600s when it comes to credit, while most clients who come to me are anywhere from the mid-400s to -500s. Depending on your goals, most clients are striving to be in what we call the 700 Club. Excellent credit is achieved at a 720 score on your credit report, but anything above 690 is good. Lenders will look at your credit score to determine the risk of lending you money. Below is the standard calculations ranges:

- **Excellent**: 720 and up. This score range is above the national average and borrowers in this field have the advantage of both getting credit approval and being offered the lowest interest rates. Lenders see low risk with only about 2% of consumers in this range becoming delinquent.

- **Very Good**: 690–720. This score identifies borrowers as highly responsible consumers and will receive lower interest rates. Lenders see a medium risk with only 8% of consumers in this range becoming delinquent.

- **Average**: 620–690. This range is identified as average. Borrowers will be able to borrow from lenders, but will have a higher interest rate than those in the 700 Club. Lenders see a medium risk here with about 28% of consumers likely to become delinquent. Note: You will likely be able to get a home mortgage or car loan, and, by continuing to repair your credit, refinance at a lower interest rate later.

- **Poor**: 560 or lower. Consumers falling within this range are considered a poor credit risk by lenders and will likely get rejected for large loans. This range often requires bigger down deposits or fees to obtain credit cards or utility services. Lenders see a high risk with about 61% of consumers below 579 likely to become delinquent.

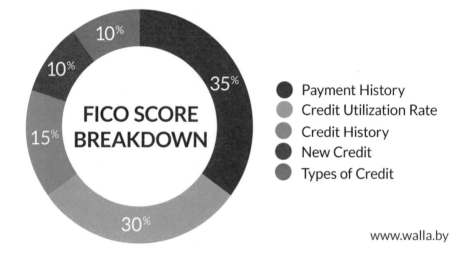

www.walla.by

5

HOW TO READ YOUR
CREDIT REPORT

I t may look confusing, but don't be intimidated by your credit report. If you are like me, or my clients, you probably thought at some point that you would always have bad credit or that it would follow you around for the rest of your life. Learning how to obtain and read your credit report will put you at ease and give you confidence.

Again, the three major credit bureaus are Experian, Equifax, and TransUnion. These three bureaus collect data from public records and companies you have chosen to do business with in order to create a personalized financial report and number to deem your creditworthiness based on a mathematical formula. Once a year, you can request a free annual credit report from www.annualcreditreport.com or by calling 877–322–8228.

Your report is divided into specific sections that require your attention, especially if you intend to dispute any errors.

1. **Personal Information**: This section includes your name (and previously used names), address (including previous addresses), social security number, and your date of birth. If you find incorrect identity information, you can write a dispute letter or notify the agency that reported the information and request that your information be updated. This is the first area to check for identity theft or perhaps inaccurate accounts applied to you from someone with the same name or a social security number that has been entered incorrectly.

2. **Employer History**: This section may be included in the personal information section. This section is typically here to help verify your identity.

3. **Account History**: This will include all of your entire financial credit history. You will find specific details on accounts, including open and closed accounts, the current status of the account, the dates that these accounts were opened/closed, joint borrower history, payment history, credit utilization, current account balances, loan payment statues, etc. This section reveals whether you are paying your accounts on time, as

well as reflects delinquent payment status. Note: Your account history is by far the most important section and will require most of your focus as it reviews an exhaustive credit list that may or may not be correct. There will undoubtedly be several errors in this section. A good example is a doctors office mistakenly reporting you neglected to pay your deductible. Disputes are the first step in repairing and rebuilding your credit, so carefully pour over every record here. Sometimes, you will find a fraudulent charge here. For example, you could see a mortgage for a house you don't own or other examples of identity theft. This will entail a deeper dispute method and reporting with the Federal Trade Commission (FTC). The Consumer Financial Protection Bureau specifically recommends watching for the following errors:

- o Accounts belonging to another person with the same name
- o Accounts created through identity theft
- o Incorrect payment history
- o Wrong balance or credit limit information
- o Reinsertion of previously corrected data

4. **Public Records**: This list includes any kind of record related to your finances, such a property liens and bankruptcies.

5. **Credit Inquiries**: This section includes anyone who has checked your credit in the past two years (landlords, employers, lenders, etc.). This is a section you can opt out of in the future, as you will learn later in the book.

6. **Inquiries**: Hard inquiries can negatively affect your credit score, but it's not the only reason to watch this section closely. A hard inquiry means a financial institution has checked your credit after someone applied for credit in your name. If you haven't authorized such an inquiry, you may keep tabs on this for identity theft.

★ ★ ★

Once you have worked on your credit report, you will notice more sections. There could be consumer statements, which would contain brief statements you have submitted to a credit bureau to dispute an item; or, if an investigation didn't resolve a dispute, this area of the statement might explain how you disagree with reported information. Once you learn how to read your credit score, it will be good practice to continually check and keep up with your financial changes each year in order to ensure the maximum points on your credit report.

6

DISPUTING TECHNIQUES

One of the terms you learned in Chapter 3 was FCRA (Fair Credit Reporting Act). This act was established to ensure that information contained in your credit report is accurate and kept confidential. This is also the law that entitles you to receive a free credit report annually. It is an important law that allows you to dispute inaccurate information on your credit report.

Note that credit disputes that are proven to be inaccurate will require the credit agency or agencies involved to correct or delete inaccurate information, which is where you come in. Most people believe you need to wait seven years to improve your credit, but you can start raising your score immediately by finding and disputing errors. At least 85% of Americans have errors unbeknownst to them on their credit reports that are negatively impacting their scores. Our experience with clients involves disputing accounts that are duplicates, inaccurately reported, outdated, and identity theft.

Removing negative information from your credit report not only puts power in your hands, but it instantly adds points to your score with just a few small steps. Account disputes can be for reasons such as deleting accounts that aren't yours, incorrect account balances, accounts paid in full, or incorrect late payments. The easiest way to begin a dispute is online. However, disputing online takes away a lot of consumer rights if the item is verified. One of those rights is the right to re-dispute it in the future. So, let's not take the easy route here. It's easy for a reason.

Online disputing has several loopholes that protect lenders over consumers. When setting up online, you will have to agree to each bureaus own terms of service, which actually takes away your rights under the FCRA. Using the automated system prevents the creation of a paper trail, which would allow you to further track results and prove any kind of agency noncompliance and even ruin your chances at a lawsuit. These terms of service also enable previously deleted items to re-report and allow reinsertion of those items into your report without any type of notification to you. Simply put, it means all the work you just did in disputing claims can come back without warning. On the other hand, mailing in a dispute letter forces them by law to give you written notice five days prior to reinsertion with adequate proof of it being legally added back to your credit file. Hard copy, snail mail methods that allow for paper trails can be tracked and, therefore, used to your advantage.

The first and most important step to disputing your credit report is asking the credit agencies to make sure that every account has been recorded accurately, completely, and legally. Accounts can remain on your credit reports for seven to ten years and many inaccuracies occur during that time. Over 85% of consumer credit reports contain errors that consumers don't know exist. You may think your credit scores are correct, but credit reporting agencies often rely on debt collectors and lenders or other data providers that furnished misinformation to investigate a dispute. Even if that data is incorrect, those inaccurate marks will remain stuck in your credit file unless you do the work yourself. When repairing my own credit, my first dispute found 42 inaccuracies and two positive accounts—my car loan and a secured credit card. Within six months, I was able to remove all 42 mistakes from my personal credit report. Bringing my FICO Scores to 783, 773, and 772.

There are several things that can hurt your credit. This would include late payments, debt collection, charge offs, repossession, foreclosure, judgments, tax liens, and bankruptcy. You could even have an error that involves your name but the wrong middle initial, leaving you responsible for the debt owed by someone else.

I have determined the most efficient process to removing inaccuracies from your report and increasing your credit score. Our steps include the following:

1. **Requesting a fresh report directly from the credit bureaus and keeping tabs on your credit reports frequently.**

   ○ IdentityIQ is a great online source for getting access to all of your credit reports to dispute errors. I personally get my three credit reports/ scores from Experian. However, they are bit more expensive. So, IdentityIQ is my second option and is actually the credit monitoring service that all of my clients use.

2. **Go over every error, large and small.**

   ○ Simple human errors can cause bad information to get stuck in your file for years to come. Here are some things to look for that can be removed or updated: credit cards that are reporting the wrong credit limits, student loans that are shown as "open" after they've been consolidated (there can even be identity theft on your report, so pay attention to everything), late payments, charge offs, bankruptcy, medical bills, collections, foreclosures, tax liens, and inquiries. If you have kept a good paper trail and track of checks and balances, you may be able to easily prove payments that were marked as late but in fact were not.

3. **Write or type your dispute letter yourself.**
   - If you need help with creating a letter, there is information in the last chapter of this book on how to get two of my dispute letters for *free*.

4. **Separate disputes for each of the three credit bureaus.**
   - You can include up to 50 accounts for each round of disputes on the same letter. You just have to separate the three credit bureaus. So, if you were disputing 50 accounts on each one of the credit bureaus, you would only need three letters. One for each bureau.

5. **Keep it simple.**
   - Don't feel the need to cite legal words or laws repeatedly. They know the laws better than you do. This makes reading your letter seem like it's coming from a law firm and not an actual consumer. Just write a brief letter that explains what accounts are in error or what information does not belong to you. For example, just say, "This account was never mine," or "These payments were never late." Also, "Please verify that this account is reporting

accurately," or "Upon reading my credit report, I found the following error(s)." Never get too specific on an account, as that may result in an update rather than a deletion. For example, do not say "I don't owe $435 on this credit card. I only owe $400." Guess what's going to happen? They're going to update it to reflect $400. Which is still negative and doesn't help your credit score at all. Simply making them aware that there is an error will suffice.

6. **Mail your dispute directly to the credit bureaus.**
   o Data furnishers are required by the Consumer Financial Protection Bureau to fully investigate any dispute brought to their attention. They have 30–45 days by law to complete their investigation. If they fail to complete the investigation in 30–45 days, the item(s) must be removed from your credit report. If the accounts cannot be verified, they must be removed from your credit report. If the account is outdated, it must be removed from your credit report. Outdated information is any account that is on your credit file for more than seven years. The time starts on the first day of your last missed payment. Bankruptcies will remain for ten years.

7. **Stay organized.**
   - Create a binder to keep track of everything related to your credit. Make copies of all of the disputes that you mail out for your personal records. Remember, your FICO Score changes over time as your credit usage and accounts change. Monitor your credit reports regularly to determine what is impacting your score. This will also help in finding fraudulent, unfair, and inaccurate marks against you.

8. **Don't accept no for an answer.**
   - Just because you made the credit bureaus aware of errors doesn't mean they miraculously come off. It is your responsibility to get all of the facts in writing and send it to all three bureaus, as well as follow up to ensure the error is corrected. Keep following up until the error is gone. Sometimes it may take five to six disputes before they finally remove the inaccuracies. They are counting on you to give up and stop disputing. Continue to use your rights under FCRA, until these items are removed.
   - There may be instances that accounts will be verified and accurately reported and you may still want to have them removed because it is hurting your credit score. A trick for that is to call the company and negotiate a smaller settlement

on the account. Once they've agreed on said settlement, get a money order or cashiers check and take a copy of it for your records. (This is the most important step, I'll explain why soon.) In the memo section, write "paid in full." This wording is extremely important. Here's why: Once you settle an account for less than the amount owed, the creditors will report the credit bureaus that you "settled for less than the amount owed," which is how it will be worded on your credit report also. But the catch is, once they cash that check or money, they agree to whatever terms that memo reads. If they don't, then they don't cash it, and it will be returned to you. Once it is cashed, you will then send that money order to the credit bureaus to show that your payment was "paid in full" as the money order/cashiers check says, not "settled for less." Therefore, by law, it must be removed because it is not being reported accurately or fairly.

7

BUILDING AND REBUILDING POSITIVE CREDIT

J ust as if you are looking to get physically fit or healthy, you need to think of getting financially healthy. There are no quick fixes in building positive credit. Just as you would gradually increase working out or eating better, you will need to apply the same discipline and mindset to get financially fabulous if you want the credit you deserve. The steps below will sound simple (and they are!), but it can be challenging to begin without the right mindset and goal. If you are wanting or needing a new home or car, then you have the goal in sight. Now you just need to take the right steps in the right direction.

Below are a few credit requirements as of 2018, just to give you an idea of where your score needs to be. As of 2018, Home Loans focuses on the FICO Base Score of 300–850. Lenders may look specifically at whether you've made rental payments on time in the past, as well as at bankruptcies and foreclosures.

- **FHA Loan**: The minimum 580 FICO Score equals a 3.5% down payment. The Federal Housing Administration (FHA) mortgage insurance program is managed by the Department of Housing and Urban Development (HUD), which is a department of the federal government. FHA loans are available to all types of borrowers, not just first-time buyers. The government insures the lender against losses that might result from borrower default. Advantage: This program allows you to make a down payment as low as 3.5% of the purchase price. Disadvantage: You'll have to pay for mortgage insurance, which will increase the size of your monthly mortgage payments.

- **VA Loan**: The United States Department of Veterans Affairs (VA) offers a loan program to military service members and their families. Similar to the FHA program, this means the VA will reimburse the lender for any losses that may result from borrower default. The primary advantage of this program—and it's a big one—is that borrowers can receive 100% financing for the purchase of a home. That means no down payment whatsoever.

- **USDA Rural Housing**: In most cases, the minimum for this loan is a 640 FICO Score. The United States Department of Agriculture (USDA) offers a loan program for rural borrowers who meet certain income requirements. The program is managed by the Rural Housing Service (RHS), which is part of the Department of Agriculture. This type of mortgage loan is offered to "rural residents who have a steady, low, or modest income, and yet are unable to obtain adequate housing through conventional financing." Income must be no higher than 115% of the adjusted area median income (AMI). The AMI varies by county.

- **Non-Prime Loans**: Loans for people with FICO Scores in the low 500s, but they require large down payments and high interest rates depending on the lender.

★ ★ ★

As of late 2017, Car Loans follow the FICO Auto Score, which is industry specific and falls in the range of 250–900. Your past behavior in this specific industry will heavily affect your score. For example, did you make late payments on previous auto loans or leases? Have you ever had a car repossessed? Have you had an auto account sent to collections? Was your car loan or lease included in your bankruptcy?

- **Prime**: 661–780 (Average APR, new car: 3.47% / Average APR, used car: 4.19%)

- **Non-Prime**: 601–660 (Average APR, new car: 4.45% / Average APR, used car: 5.94%)

- **Subprime**: 501–600 (Average APR, new car: 12.14% / Average APR, used car: 16.72%)

- **Deep Subprime**: 300–500 (Average APR, new car: 14.93% / Average APR, used car: 19.51%)

Note: Anything under a 500 credit score will be a red flag to a lender. However, if you can prove that you have a stable job and can make a substantial down payment like I did, it is possible to get a car loan. Be prepared to document your ability to pay bills on time for at least six months, as well as have an explanation ready regarding any other issues that may have popped up on your report. Even though your interest rate will not be where you want it, you can still use the steps in this book to raise and refinance your loan later for a lower interest rate, which will likely provide immediate relief to the tune of a couple hundred bucks a month.

★ ★ ★

As you can see, a higher credit score will save you tons of money and lower your interest rates. One of the first steps I took before disputing inaccuracies was getting an unsecured credit card. This aids in building positive credit as the inaccuracies are being disputed and removed. Using your credit cards responsibly is a great way to build your credit and can make a big difference in which bracket your scores goes into.

Credit utilization makes up a big chunk (30%) of your credit score. Your credit utilization rate is the amount of debt you have compared to your total available credit. If you don't ever get a credit card, you are easily leaving up to 120 points on the table—a huge mistake when it comes to establishing better credit. While you can potentially reach the credit score you want without a credit card, it will undoubtedly take at least two to three times longer to make up for over 100 points when you leave a huge category like this unchecked on your credit report card.

There are a few tricks to taking care of your credit card that will ensure you reach adding the maximum number of points to your credit score. Remember in Chapter 4 when we discussed how FICO Scores are determined? The greatest impact on your credit scores is payment history. You can positively affect your credit score simply by paying your bills on time, all the time. That being said, late or missed payments also negatively affect credit scores. When repairing and building credit, sometimes it's just a few more points that will push you into a new tier, so I have personally tested these techniques to get even more out of your credit card payments.

The traditional way of thinking is that paying your credit card off increases your credit score the most because you don't owe anyone anything. But many people are unaware that FICO actually calculates a $0 balance as a 30% utilization. This means that you need to carry at least a 1% to 7% balance to calculate the sweet spot of having the lowest utilization. In short, you do not get credit for maintaining a zero balance. That does not look like maintaining credit to a lender. Your credit card company wants to feel like they are able to make interest off of you, so as awful as it sounds, a zero balance actually does more harm than keeping a low amount on your credit card. A good example of this is if you have a credit card with a $1,000 limit and you owe $500, you will have a 50% utilization rate. A good credit-to-debt ratio is considered less than 30%. (Again, zero equals thirty percent!) That's where my own tricks come in to beat the system at its own game.

Understanding how to read your credit card statement will help you reach the 1% utilization. There are two important elements to note: One is the due date and the other is the statement date. The due date is, of course, the date payment is due, but the statement date is actually the date your balance is reported to the credit bureaus. This reporting date always comes after the payment date. Let's say you don't want to pay interest, and your due date is June 1 with the statement date being June 4. You would pay everything off by June 1 but put a small purchase (even if it is just a couple of dollars) on the card before June 4. This trick ensures you have paid off your debt in full while also ensuring you are reported for a 1% utilization rather than the 30% utilization that comes with a zero balance. This is something I have played around with considerably to make sure that it actually works. While the credit points are nothing drastic, it can be the difference between having a 714 but needing to raise your credit score six extra points to a 720, or a 636 to a 640, which would give you a completely different interest rate by putting you in a different credit bracket. Implementing these tricks each month is a wonderful way to beat the credit system at its own game because you're not paying interest, and you're still getting the maximum amount of points.

Another tip is to keep your credit card balances low and not apply for any credit while disputing unless it's absolutely necessary. Applying for new lines of credit while disputing will cause your credit score to drop. It can be discouraging to see your score drop while you're working to increase it, so once the dispute process is over, then you can begin to apply for new lines of credit and see the progress as you head into areas like getting a mortgage or buying a car.

Below are things that drop your credit score and should never be done, especially when building or restoring credit, if it can be helped:

1. **Making a late payment:** This has the most significant impact on your credit score. Any late payments of more than 30 days will be reported to the credit bureaus and will be immediately reflected in your score.

2. **Maxing out your credit cards:** You can lose 100-plus points by maxing out your credit cards, making it impossible to track how much your credit score increases if your utilization is working against you.

3. **Applying for credit:** This is also known as a hard inquiry and can immediately drop your score anywhere between 5–50 points. Getting unsecured credit cards to build credit isn't always easy with poor or nonexistent credit history. If that is the case for you, a secured credit card might be the best option. I highly recommend using this secured card because of the guaranteed approval rate (with the exception of being in bankruptcy), and the success that I've seen my clients have by using it responsibly (www.creditbuildercard.com/ampmcredit.html).

8

CALL TO ACTION

Each person that comes to me is different. Sometimes there may not be anything to dispute because all of information is being reported accurately, which is rare. I have clients that only need 60–90 days to repair their credit, and I have clients who need to stay in the program for six months to over a year. Point being, everyone's journey in repairing their credit will be different. What may take you six months to achieve could take someone else 45 days, since no two credit files are identical. Results will always vary.

Most of our clients want a mortgage, so their goal is always to achieve a 580–700 credit score. While you can get a mortgage at 580, you will get a much more favorable interest rate from your lenders once you reach 640 and higher. So I always say we strive for you to reach a goal of being in the 700 Club.

While the techniques are fully explained, this is a process that requires time and effort. I want you to have this information at your fingertips so you can do this yourself. There is no quick fix to restoring or building credit, but this is a process that works. Also, I know sometimes you have school, a job, kids, or all of the above and need someone else do the work for you.

This book was created for those who have the time, organizational skills, and discipline to keep up with the credit repair process. If you've finished this book and realized that this is just too much for you to figure out on your own, that's OK too. Many people know that they can repair their credit themselves, but they just don't have the time to do so.

If you have more questions or feel overwhelmed by the process, schedule a free consultation with AM/PM Credit Repair through our website at www.ampmcredit.com, so that we can see how we can help you become one of our next praise reports. We know what works! Remember, after using AM/PM Credit Repair, the difference in your credit will be like day and night!

9

CHANGING
STEREOTYPES

There are so many stereotypes associated with bad credit that just aren't true. As a society in general, we aren't openly given the tools to become financially successful, simply because it doesn't make lenders money. Money and credit can also be a taboo subject to talk about, so if you don't know, you just don't know. Don't let that stop you from learning now.

One of the biggest stereotypes people with bad credit face is that they are not responsible or that they don't pay their bills. A lot of the time, it has absolutely nothing to do with either of those issues. Your credit score is not your character or your income level. I have clients who come to me because their homes burned down or because they've lost everything due to natural disasters, divorces, or from being laid off at a job they had been at for over ten years and are therefore unable to make a couple of months rent or mortgage. Maybe you don't have health insurance and have huge medical bills.

Life happens, and you don't have to be ashamed of what is out of your control. One of my jobs is to educate people about these stereotypes and let them know there is nothing to be ashamed about. There could be a million reasons or one really good reason why your credit score isn't where you want it to be, but we can change that. It is definitely not your fault if you know nothing about credit scores, it's because it isn't something anyone wants to tell us. Believe me, it is easier and much more beneficial for lenders to keep you in the dark about restoring or building your credit.

I hope to change that with this book and with AM/PM Credit Repair, and I know you do too if you are reading this. You don't have to hold a college degree or a special title to take control of your financial health. It is up to us to share the knowledge we have to help others and even to encourage others to keep us accountable. Often, poor credit is associated with a cycle of debt you cannot get out from under, which leads to anxiety, worry, and hopelessness with no end of the road in sight.

If you are still on the fence or feeling apprehensive about building your credit, you are not alone in that either. Studies show that African Americans and Latinos are deemed "credit invisible" because of a lack of credit history. This is simply because of insufficient credit history to generate a credit score. Two of the biggest reasons these groups don't have higher credit is because they feel they have no reason to build credit (40%) and they don't know how to check or build their credit (35%). Building the life you want and deserve is reason enough.

After going through the steps in this book, you now know you do have a reason to build credit, and you have the tools to do it directly. Build your confidence by using the steps in this book and see how quickly you can add points to your score.

You can even build your child's credit profile without them knowing it by setting your child or family up as an authorized user on your credit card. They don't even have to know about this. You would be able to gift this to your kids as young adults whenever you feel they are responsible enough to handle this information. You didn't know anything about credit, but imagine being able to give your kids a credit score of 750 as a birthday or graduation gift! Awesome, right? If you maintain a healthy financial record, that will translate to your child's profile and set them up for success when they enter the real world and begin looking at private school loans, car loans, or their own credit cards or mortgages.

Remember, it is not the end of the world if you have bad credit. In fact, millions of Americans across the board are rated well below average. You can go from coach to first class just by educating yourself. It's important to know that bad credit won't stay with you forever. With just a little discipline, you too can become a success story.

10

SUCCESS STORIES

A gain, having poor credit is not the end of the world, even though it may seem like it right now. You may think it's not realistic to go from a low 400 credit score to a 700 credit score in a few months, but that's because you have never been given the right tools to get there. It is absolutely possible, and it's absolutely possible for you to do it yourself, if you have the time and desire to take these steps.

I don't have any college degrees or titles, but I dug into learning as much as I could online and from professionals. I then tested these methods on myself, so I now know that they work. I'm just a regular person who decided to figure it out on my own, and I want other people to know that if I can do this, then they can do this too. Remember that your success is my success. Don't take my word for it, read some of our reviews from real clients about how their lives and credits were transformed with the help of AM/PM Credit Repair.

★ ★ ★

"I made my fiance, who is a merchant seaman on the boat currently, wake up at 2:00 a.m. on January 30th to sign up for a free consultation because he was so frustrated with where his score was. I referred him to Ashley Massengill at AM/PM Credit Repair because I knew she was the truth! And less than a month later, his score went up 116 points. Thank you so much, Ashley, for helping us!" —Courtney Henderson (TransUnion: 751 Excellent; Equifax 748 Good; up a total of 116 points in 30 days)

"I started with AM/PM last year in December 2017, and, no, it hasn't been a quick fix, but it is definitely money well spent. I have followed all the advice Ashley and her team have put together for me, and my credit has gone up over 100 points. I'm very close to being able to purchase my first home. Thanks to Ashley! She's very good at what she does. You won't regret it! The level of professionalism they provide to you is beyond exceptional. I wouldn't choose anyone else to repair my credit." —Driaa Monique

"I can not thank you enough for all the help. Today, on my birthday, I received notice that we will close on our home on

May 22nd. Thank you, guys, for all the help. I will be watching out for your next training academy. I will be there. You guys are amazing." —Latise Williams

"Becoming a member of the AM/PM family was one of the *best* decisions I could have made. Eleven deletions in one month. All praises to God, the lovely Mrs. Ashley Massengill, and her wonderful crew." —Diamond Shavon

"I started AM/PM on March 20th. My credit score was 549. I checked my FICO Score this morning, and it has increased 100 points! My goal was to put myself in a position where I would be eligible to purchase a home some time this year. With the score I have now, I know it is possible, so I went ahead and signed up for a First-time Home Buyer Workshop on May 19th. I know I'm not done, but I'm well on my way. Ashley Massengill, you are a blessing, and I am thankful for your company's hard work on my behalf." —DeDe Johnson

"I signed up with Ashley last year. She told me my credit was 'not really bad,' but she could help make it a little better. I know for sure I got on her nerves. I texted, I called, I emailed. I had so many questions. But what did she do? She texted, called, and emailed me back, answering each one. I came to her with a score of 640–645. She worked her magic for only 30 days, and I closed on my new home with a 710. May not be much to y'all, but I am forever grateful. Not only did she help my score increase, but she gave me tips on how to keep it up! I love her for that!" —Sean Watson

"I can't say enough positive things about my experience with AM/PM Credit Repair! Excellent, custom service with real results, quickly! I love this company!" —Tygia Clayton

"My wife and I jumped onboard at the beginning of the year and wished we had jumped onboard sooner. AM/PM cares about their clients. We joined in February, applied for a mortgage this month (July), and are currently closing on our mortgage! That says enough about AM/PM!" —Joshua Wade Sr.

"OK, so I've been saying I wanted to get my credit together because I'll be 25 this year, and I need to start adulting. I started following Ashley Massengill about eight months ago because I saw that she does amazing things with credit repair. I was apprehensive at first, but after seeing a multitude of her praise reports, I decided to take the leap. She's not even done, and I've only been her client for 30 days, and my TransUnion report went up 122 points! Experian went up 125 points! Mind you, she's not even done yet! I had three derogatory marks and *all* have been deleted. She and her team are amazing at what they do. If you need credit repair, she's the go-to. Also, #supportblackownedbusinesses #blackgirlmagic" —Olivia Nicole

★ ★ ★

Want more information?

Social Media: www.facebook.com/ampmcredit
Website: www.ampmcredit.com

To receive two of my dispute letters for *free*, for your own personal use, please send an email to ashley@firstclasscredit. com. Please include the code "ampm" to prove that you purchased this book to receive your letters.

StoryTerrace®